THIRD EYE
AWAKENING

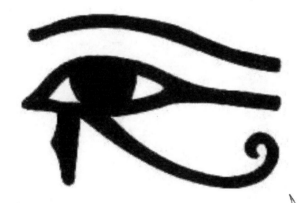

THERONE
SHELLMAN

To: Delores
Be Blessed!
11.01.2016

Order Books At:

www.amazon.com/author/theroneshellman

IG:
FB: Therone Shellman Media

Authors Note

Some may take this work as an attack on their personal beliefs. Yet time has shown that all Truths are meant to be tried and tested. Growth is inevitable. Whether humans are ready or not, days will come and all things are continually becoming. Tomorrow is at the mercy of what happens today. Always seek the truth no matter the opposition. Like an atom positive and negative both adhere to one omnificent order. No power within this physical world is greater than the One which holds all things in balance.

ISBN: 10-1480039012
ISBN: 13-978-1480039018

Typeset by Anita Davies, for Anita Davies Editing
Edited by English Ruler, ARC Book Club, Inc.

This book is dedicated to all the spirits seeking greater understanding of their existence.

CONTENTS

INTRODUCTION

Dare to dream, hope, believe, seek, feel, find, and love.

- Mike Hull

Change your thoughts and you change the world.

- Norman Vincent Peale

Is. Dolores Kortright   Ms. Dolores Kortright

For success, attitude is equally as important as ability.

- Harry F. Banks

If you find that thing you love, it doesn't necessarily matter whether you do it well or not – you just need to do it.

- Stanley Tucci

PLUS
THE POWER OF FAITH

PLUS
THE POWER OF FAITH

Spirituality and religion are quite different. Spirituality is dealing with life beyond the physical realms and equating all things within life and all worlds to one source that permeates through all plains of existence. Spirituality is the reality of the Oneness of All.

For over twenty years, the author has travelled the roads of disappointment, confusion and despair to find peace and happiness. And it is through experience that he truly gained the wisdom to write this book, which is clearly an explanation of the human mind and the mind of the Creator.

The purpose of this work is solely to explore truth in all its degrees without prejudice. Humans must rise above the chains that bind them in order to truly witness eternal peace. There is no boogie man or evil besides that which humans harbor within themselves which ultimately serves as mankind's foe. Humans are the only enemies mankind faces. And it is the mortal mind which is the only true enemy of man/woman. It's not until an individual frees himself or herself from individuality and personality and all the vices and bad virtues they both harbor that one can reach the most high in consciousness and within themselves as well.

11

The Creator is the Lord of All the Worlds (material and non-material). All things are manifested through this one omnificent power. And it is in all creations that the Creator dwells. There is no need to be saved because, all life is eternal. Energy doesn't die it transforms itself from one stage to another.

The journey of each human in this physical realm is to add on to the Creators Plan in the up building of this world. All that you see around you is the vision of the Creator manifested to Man.

All that which is of progress is the vision of the Creator. All things were created to progress. It is Self not the Higher Conscious of Man which seeks to alter this. Individuality and Personality seek to separate the Oneness of all life. All things are One.

THE AWAKENING

"I assure you that who you see in the mirror is not your true self. It is a mere image, and images are illusions based upon human perception and mortal mind. This moment in time is but only a moment. This physical existence is but only a stage of development in the realms of many lives you've lived and are to live. For an eternity you shall either rise to perfection, or suffer at the hands and deeds of your own doing."

WAKE UP!

The fear of death is man's greatest obstacle. Conquer your fear and you will conquer death.

Fear not the end because, it will never come.

Energy doesn't die it transforms itself from one stage to another. There is no such thing as death for man or any living creature for the Creator is within man, and all living things within all planes of nature. There is no need to be saved for the spirit is eternal. Every soul is unique, imprisoned within a physical body. Through life's labor each soul engages in its great work to free itself from the limitations of the mortal mind and this physical world and become one with the Divinity.

The mastering of oneself is man's greatest task. One which will allow him to serve his maker and brethren without prejudice and limitation. Envy, lust, greed, hate, fear, ambition, and personalities are the obstacles all men/women face within themselves to move past the limitations of mortal mind. None shall rise above human ignorance who fail to conquer these to seek the temple where the creator dwells, where the eternal truth shines.

"At the age of twenty-eight I became faced with making the decision as to where I wanted to take my life. Up to this point all I'd known was monetary success overruled by the ever-present reality of possible imprisonment. I suffered at the hand of my own choices and actions. I was my worst enemy because I placed my desires and wants above my own well-being. But my luck was running out. Realizing this I decided I needed to take control of my mind, and thoughts so I can produce different conditions and circumstances."

Man is elder to all the kingdoms of nature. Plant, animal and minerals along with man are all one. And it is not until man recognizes his duty and obligation to serve from what he has gained from The creator can he truly understand the oneness of life, no matter the form of energy or plane.

The light of the creator exists in all things, and all are bound to one universal order and principle. No one thing exists in isolation or apart from the next. All life

matter serves in spiritual unity within the universe no matter the plane.

All men who have reached within themselves to stomp out ignorance and embrace the temple of the creator within themselves respect all religions. But yet hold dear to none. The Son of Man, the Creators son, the conscious recognizes that all religions derive from one story told in diverse ways for people from different regions and beliefs.

The three modern religions, Buddhism, Christianity and Islam all owe their beginning to schools of thought and principles birthed from the higher schools of learning in Egypt. And thus the Egyptians owe the founding of their institutions and thinking to Ethiopia and so on.

Three thousand years before the tenants of Christianity the story of the "Holy Ghost" appears in Egyptian fables. Through a series of events and murdered by his brother Typhon, the spirit of Osiris visits Isis and she gives birth to a son who they name Harpocrates. It is here that the story of the Immaculate Conception in Christianity was formed.

"When I was fifteen years old I was introduced to the teachings of "Nation of Gods and Earths" which was called back then "Five Percent Nation". One of their core beliefs is that man is the maker and master of his circumference and destiny. Each of us is a god unto ourselves under the one universal power, which is the lord of all worlds. Later I came to see this truth derived straight out of Egyptian thinking and history before any modern belief."

There is no need or cause to believe in miracles, for somewhere in nature there is a cause for every effect. Even though there are many effects that we do not understand through mortal mind. All cause inherently lies in the mental and metaphysical plane before manifesting themselves within the physical plane.

The modern world recognizes new born beliefs such as Christianity, Buddhism and Islam. Yet reject the religions and philosophical ideals of past civilizations they were the product of.

Plato, Aristotle, Socrates and other recognized and highly respected European thinkers have admitted openly that the western thinking of their time was no match, and below in standard to that of the antiquity of African schools of learning and persons of scholarly nature for that matter. Most modern scientists, religious scholars and philosophical thinkers have established their beliefs upon hollow ground and in arrogance they fail to retrace the steps of man back to the beginning. Or at least back to the earliest times of written and recorded history. In doing so they turn their back on eternal truth. They gaze upon half-truths and wonder. Their mortal mind and personality blind them.

From the Egyptians it is noted that the human soul is immortal. This truth was revealed to Solon who was the first of the great Athenian law-givers and one of the highest respected thinkers of the Greeks. Yet he and Plato who later followed into Egypt acknowledge that the Egyptians considered the Greeks children in learning. Therefore not all was revealed to them. Nor did the states religion of Egypt reveal all the mysteries of the first Cause that brought life into being for the universe, including the birth of man. The ancient priests were under oath as sworn protectors of the truth, so it is evident they carefully concealed deeper truths from the uninitiated. That is those who weren't students of the mysteries and higher schools of learning.

"After twenty plus years of study I've come to the realization that concealing of the deeper truths from the average individual even takes place today. This is so even in the church, other religious schools and fraternal organizations. The average person in the congregation knows the general beliefs of the institution. While the

19

deeper truths are only revealed to those who seek and take the initiative to move further into the circle of influence reserved for the higher thinkers of their faith or doctrine. As a Five Percenter even as teen, my thirst for knowledge moved me amongst those who were respected for their insight into the deeper truths of our faith. My quest for the truth didn't stop there though. At the age of twenty-eight, I made the conscious decision to move on from the Nation, deciding it was necessary to separate myself from the label, faiths, doctrines, individuality and personality. Truth is impersonal and does not belong to any individual or group of individuals solely. It is universal and belongs to all."

All who seek the truth be mindful for it is deep within the mind where all truths lie.

"Know Thy Self" are the words that have echoed for thousands of years from those far greater in understanding than ourselves. These words tell the story of what road a man must take to find the most illustrious riches a man can encounter. It is within oneself that the flames of eternity light up the temple of the most high.

Seek for the glory of ambition and one will trek upon the road to ruin. All the history of man stands before us as testament to show that ambition is the cause for men to plot on one another such as Typhon and Osiris, Caine and Abel. It is the reason men desire riches, power and sovereignty.

The effect is steering humanity away from its ultimate goal of becoming one with the Creator.

Ambition is also the cause of ignorance, superstition, fear and personality. Personality is the undoer of all men.

Today we have reached a point in thinking where knowledge is the common property of mankind. Yet there are many who seek to rule others because, of their ignorance.

In the past knowledge and learning was under the lock and key of a few chosen individuals as it was thought to be of great privilege to become a member of the Mystery Schools of Sacred Institutions of education. This was done to protect the common man from learned individuals who were of bad character and virtue, so their greed and ambition did not undermine the progress of the community. In today's setting, many of the learned have betrayed their duty to act in good faith according to the most upheld principles and virtues. Instead of serving the most High they serve Self, and in doing so they threaten to undermine the equality of humans and all other life forms.

"In elevating in my studies and spiritual awareness I've come to realize that religion is personality, no different from an individual being given a name at birth. It's a name, a title which separates you from everyone else. The truth is universal, in and a part of all. Christians believe their truth is greater than Muslims truth; the Muslims feel the same toward the Christians. Both speak of one Creator. I remember as a Five Percenter being outspoken against and discriminatory to those who weren't as if I was better than they were. The fact that I didn't look at the Creator as being something outside of myself didn't make me any different from them. My lack of tolerance was all about Self not the Creator."

The first duty of all those who seek truth is to discipline their thoughts.

You must welcome all good and discard the idea of negative thinking. Your mind must also be guarded against the intrusion or invasion of others thinking. By mastering oneself, one masters the world outside.

Be of certainty that all who you allow into your confidence and all you bestow wisdom upon are worthy.

Do not give advice, especially of a spiritual nature to those who will not use it. To reveal knowledge to those who are sinful is equivalent to handing them explosives. All who ask must be worthy of knowing, and earn the right to obtain.

You do all the above to ensure you do not assist those ruled by ambition to further their cause. On a daily basis spiritual values are set aside so individuals can hunt down power, wealth, status and fame. All for the sake of depriving or dethroning others.

If thou seek to become a wise man, one must undertake the cause of up building within themselves and the outer world. One must be active in building a better world for the glory of the Creator.

"When I decided to change my life from being reckless to myself and toward others I made a pact with myself that instead of destroying, I would seek to build. Through my writing I would enlighten others to help them think and live a better life. This in turn would help build a better world."

One does not enter the state of wickedness by the road of fate or circumstance but by the thoughts they choose and the actions they take because of desires. A good man does not become wicked by mere mishap of ill fortune. Negative thoughts have lain dormant within his mind and heart for quite some time aching to be manifested. We do not become that of which we want without being of that. Nor do we attract what we want but instead call to us that which we are.

Your thoughts and actions can either serve to imprison you, or liberate you with the greater cause and eternal truth.

We are set free or chained by our thoughts. The right thoughts can serve to build you up into divinity; by abusive thoughts we fall to the level of animal nature.

Man is the master of his own fate. This is so even in the weakest condition. He can abuse his mind and body and be of poor condition. Even so, he is still the master of his own fate.

Unfortunately, man makes foolish decisions that only serve to cause them more harm when they're in the weakest moments. When man comes to understand the rules that govern thought he can meditate upon such types of thinking and apply these laws to his benefit.

Each soul beholds its own life and individuality, yet is connected to one eternal truth. By digging deep into ones consciousness an individual will stumble upon all truth attached to their being.

Through patience and diligent search one will be enriched with the understanding of themselves and walk upon the threshold of the temple of Eternal truth.

"From my early teens to late twenties, over and over I constantly inflicted pain upon myself. Hustling and chasing fast money and opportunity constantly landed me in prison and overpowered me with a sense of not being free or safe. There was not a second of the day where I didn't think about watching my back. At the age of twenty-eight I came to the realization that I'm the master of my own fate, and whatever good or bad comes my way is brought about by my own doing. I can be my own best friend, or my own worst enemy. I've always been into reading and educating myself. Now at this point I was ready to start applying everything I'd learned. It was from all my past negative experiences that I developed the roughness I needed to able to handle obstacles and setbacks. There was no doubt to be felt because my fate is what I will. If I desired a better life then all I had to do was think and act desirable thoughts and actions."

Love for the material, small attitudes and the lust for wealth, worldly power diminish a man's ability to reach greatness. For it's not in emotions and possessions that a man's greatness is found, but it is within his beliefs, virtues and duty to the Creator, nature and fellow man that a man goes about his labor in a great way. And through this doing greatness is achieved. When men come together under such union, there is nothing that cannot be accomplished for the good of all human families. While it is also man's dabbling in excessive emotions and the desire to possess that of the world which has crumbled some of man's greatest achievements.

A man who masters the world within himself will surely learn to master the outer world.

The physical world is but a reflection of the spiritual world. Mind and body both bare witness to a higher reality, which is the law giver to all forms of life which follow the same rules. Each plane just being an extension of the next, appearing but never existing on its own accord.

In order for peace to exist between all men there must be a common understanding that all men are entitled the same rights, liberties and ability to rise forth into greatness. There can be no prejudices whatsoever. This common ideology must be shared in order for the physical world of humans to be secure in peace. Without brotherhood, all that man does and accomplishes amounts to a grain of sand upon a beach.

Without unity our greatest accomplishment will remain nothing in the eyes of our Creator, for the Common law of all things are Love and Unity.

"Since I was young I've been afflicted with many prejudices and ignorance against myself and others.

Distrust of others revealed the lack of trust I harbored for myself. And most are infected with the same bug, personality and individuality rule dimming the light of eternal truth within ourselves and that which we see in others. It's this fear which hinders humans from getting past mistakes.

Repeatedly we return to that point of pain. I decided my writings would help me seek the deeper truths to build the house within. And in doing so I would enable others to do the same."

The growth of humans is a natural occurrence. Nothing can alter the

development of Cause and Effect in the physical, spiritual and mental realms.

It is when a human becomes spiritually conscious that they are more aware of their thoughts, and possess more of a need to control their mind. They realize by controlling their mind, they have power over their thoughts and actions. Thus, one has more of a probability of obtaining positive results time after time.

Circumstances are the result of that which your soul harbors. It attracts that which it fears, loves and desires. What one faces in the outer world for good or bad affects ones inner self and thought.

Whether we become dominated by circumstances, or rise above that which we reaped from sowing all depends on whether one accepts the fact they are the makers of their own destiny.

It's important to set aside one hour or two for self, so that you can meditate and ponder about past thoughts and actions, present thoughts and actions needed to be taken. Concentrate on your journey and the lessons learned. Focus on how all you've encountered has made you a better person. Have you found that which the Creator wants you to? If not then think about the paths you've taken upon your search. Meditate on that which you can do for our Creator and your fellow humans. On the other hand if you've already found your duty "have you begun to labor tirelessly for the good of all"? Or have you been a victim of personality and individuality undoing all you undertake for the sake of vanity, fame and acknowledgement? There is no need to do any ritual, cross hands or feet. All that's needed is some time alone to think and reflect.

"I've always been a thinker. It's one reason why I never got into using drugs or boozing heavily.

Both of these alter your thinking capacity greatly. Some people have said to me over the years that I think too much as if it's a bad thing. Whereas I feel it's a very good thing because, looking back upon my life, I see that I've made it through all the impossibilities because of thinking. I was not raised by my mother and father, instead I was shuffled through the foster care system. And as a result I learned life the hard way taking my bumps and scrapes, bandaging myself up the best way I could and moving on. It was important to move on, but without spiritual awareness I was basically a blind man walking into walls. After years of sitting down and talking to myself I got within, dug deep and the way was revealed to me. I not only had to talk right, I had to be right. In other words I needed to think and live positively."

That which is outside of yourself does not possess power until you see places or things as being powerful. Either you can be controlled by that which is outside of you, or you can control it.

People are not included in this argument because each soul has its own purpose and no other soul should trespass upon the path of another. So stay clear of seeking to control your fellow humans.

Happiness is already within humans, as well as it is all throughout the universe vibrating brightness like sunshine. To search outside of oneself for a treasure which one already possesses is a futile act. Our Creator is Love, and in creating all, everything that he is exists within all his creations.

Do not waste your time with gossip, or conversations that aren't constructive in relation to you or others. Seek to speak nicely of others, and guard your thoughts whenever negative thoughts abound in relation to others. Admire, but never be a groupie to those caught up in the illusions of fame. Think not of their accomplishment, for all humans have the same capabilities to find an occupation or labor that they can excel at above others. All souls have a definite purpose which is different from all others. When one taps into this purpose, they seem to others to be extraordinary and worthy of idolization. It is your purpose to find your own purpose and you should waste no time in foolish talk about what others are doing. This is especially so when the paths you both trek do not cross one another, as to assist each other in the labor you undertake for the Creator and fellow humans.

"I myself respect the talent and drive of others, but idolization is something I stay away from. Master P and Jay Z are my two of favorite hip-hop icons. Not so much for their music but more so for their business savvy and ability to be leaders and innovators in their field. Kelly Rowland and Alicia Keyes, both beautiful women with extraordinary singing capabilities and beauty, have attracted me. Not so much for their talents but more so for how down to earth and humble they are in the midst of all the fame and hoopla. The glamour and glitter of the outside world has not dimmed the light and beauty within. In my personal career, I stay clear of the shining lights. I view myself as just an ordinary person doing extraordinary things. Whenever I run into someone seeking to throw praise upon me, I make sure to remind them that we're all meant to do great things. The only difference between others and myself is I'm doing what I can instead of just talking about it."

Do all you can do and never procrastinate. Make the most of every second of time, for there isn't one second to waste or spare. Time is but a mere illusion based on what humans have termed it to be reflecting the knowledge and understanding of science they possess. One day can seem to be many. While weeks and months can seem to be only one day. Your talent is for you, and you alone, and it will feed and clothe you if you pursue it. But first you must take time and care to learn and become proficient in your labor so you can get the most out of it and serve the world in a great way.

"Writing a book has always been a goal of mine since I was around sixteen. I used to write girls letters in junior high school and they loved them. So you can say that writing has been and is a passion of mine. And it is something I do well. Therefore, it's no wonder as to why I chose writing as a profession once I decided to get my life together. It took me two decades later to complete my dream of having a book published. Nevertheless, I did it. And the whole while I never concerned myself with other writers or the industry. My only thought was composing a story that readers would learn from and be entertained by. "Love Don't Live Here" my first was published years ago and now I'm the author of several books. At one time I even had the pleasure of publishing others. This experience is over but nevertheless I'm an author who continuously releases a new title every year."

Never overly concern yourself with failure. If you trip and stumble then pick yourself up and keep going.

Failures for the thinking and doing individual are but temporary, even if temporary failure is revisited more than once. Success is a thinking and doing man's/woman's reward. Sooner or later the road will be paved and a path created from all the trekking and hard work.

Be a willing student, for those who seek must also be willing to learn. Knowledge, wisdom and understanding are but tools built from sacrifice, study and life experience. The glory of your work and accomplishments will show as proof to your virtue and dedication to knocking on the Creators door to serve.

All that you experience you'll walk with for the rest of your life. Every time you move past an obstacle, win a victory, lose a battle, fall and stumble your subconscious records for you to remember. It is from this point that you become that which you think about most. If you see yourself as failing, then you in turn welcome failure as an ultimate destination point you and all of who you are. Your whole existence will be a failure because this is what you believe yourself to be. Now if you believe that ultimately your temporary failures build a path to success then you affirm that good because you're of good is yours to have. It's just the process of learning and doing that, which will bring it to you permanently.

If you seek success, wealth and prosperity and wish to not give up individuality and personality all that you gain today will ultimately be lost in the days to come. That which is not built in love has no foundation. All houses built from the top to bottom shall surely crumble. Our Creator is Love and all things sought and built through him are possible. While the man dwelling in self-love may acquire through mortal mind that which he acquires he cannot keep for all things built with emotions are unstable. It is only through the Creators understanding that creations and services serve unselfishly within his plan and that of all fellow humans, animals and nature.

"Who I am today has everything to do with who I was yesterday along with past experiences and the knowledge gained through it all. Today I have good thoughts about who I am, and because I think this way about myself my confidence level in regards to what I can do and accomplish is sky high. As a teen and into my twenties consciously I felt I was a young man with a lot of talent and ambition that was a bit powerless because of restrictions I really thought were hindering me from progressing.

1. I was on parole.
2. I didn't have any real family support.
3. I was a young African American male with a felony.

All these things led me to believe the world was against me in some way. Since my central thoughts focused on the negative I acted this out by selling drugs and committing other crimes.

I did all this when it probably would have just took a little more effort to go out and get a job. At twenty-eight years old, I decided to make clean break and change my life. I at once took control of my mind, thoughts and ultimately my actions. Like clockwork, I began to obtain different results, and as a result my self-confidence began building until I came to the point where I was secure with myself, and fixed on the thought that we are what we think."

Without prejudice, seek the truth. Whether it's within a child, woman, man or institution think not of the bearer but the focus on the light.

Acknowledge the truth in all its forms and realities. Our Creator is within us all like a flashlight illuminating the darkness. Seek the brightness in all for it exists, at some points out in the open, and at others hidden encased or clothed by that which blinds the average.

"A little after my early teens I began to really question my own existence and that of our Creators. It never made sense to me to think of the Creator as an entity outside of man. Especially if I was under the understanding that the Creator is within all things and man is created in his image and likeness. One of my friends' older brothers was a member of the Five Percent Nation. And he was someone I respected so I decided to take a close look.

One of the core beliefs of the nation is that man has the ability to control his own conditions and circumstances. Every individual has the ability to master his or her mind, spirituality and body. We all are the makers of our own destiny. Each man is a god unto himself, for our Creator is supreme mind and the lord of all worlds. I grew up in the church so the views of the nation in many ways conflicted with everything I was taught up to this point. But I was open to seeking and because of this I was able to see the bigger picture. Even in the Bible it speaks about Man being created in Gods image and likeness. The Creator in essence, is of non-material matter and so is man. It's through thought that the Creator lives through man on this physical plain.

The path to enlightenment is a rough road. When you think you've made progress and some success the table more than likely will be turned on you.

Out of nowhere, repeated failure will show its ugly a face once again and from this experience you'll have something to learn from. Your suffering will seem unfair as if you're being punished unjustly. You may even misunderstand the lessons to be gained through all of this. What doesn't break you will ultimately make you. Only the unbroken shall have the strength to endure all that awaits because it is through all the hurdles, road blocks, setbacks and pain that one reaches beyond the gates of the world where all is understood to be things to learn from and move past so that once again peace within can be restored and peace outside can be witnessed. You were created in peace, and as a child you learned to create war within yourself, and you manifested it into the outer world. When you let go of self like a child once again you will not fear. It is then that you will come to know the Creator.

37

Excess in emotions is the product of man's mortal mind. One must rise above their beastly desires in order to enter the depths of infinite conscious.

Anger, hatred, jealousy, envy, lust, vanity, pride and self-indulgence are all mortal sins which bring you further outside of yourself.

Men engage in long arguments, construct treatise, scriptures and many books yet most know not the truth. Those who know the truth are those who live it. The patient, calm, forgiving, unbiased manifest the truth in all they think and do. It is these virtues that belong to the Creator. Love is the Creator and Love is within all his creations.

"I remember the days as a teen and twenty something year old debating with others over religious, spiritual and political ideals. In some cases these heated debates turned into arguments. In other instances they lead to more talks. It was this environment, which forged my ambition to learn. The stronger I became in arguing my point the more I hit the books.

Yet I've always been under the belief that the possession of knowledge alone does not make a man right. It is his thoughts combined with action that determine who he really is. This determines if he's Gods son, or the son of his own demons and ignorance. A man of good virtue is farther along the road of truth than an intellectual, who's well read or possesses many degrees, but who is not a friend to man or the world".

Talk without action is meaningless. Heated debates about truth serve no purpose. Rather than talk about truth, think truth and live it. Practice patience and love. Search your heart, mind and soul for the light which will free you. Those who know truth do not belong to any special religion or doctrine. Therefore, there is no need to convert or belong to any group whether of special doctrine or fraternity. True believers are the saviors of the human race and stand in-between the enslaved and the Creator.

Individuals who are self-centered and deny others the goodness they receive bring about hatred, jealousy and many other dreams. They look upon others as savages, unlearned, infidels, and wicked and in doing so render all their thoughts and actions to be null and void. Truth is not limited to any individual or special group. There is no truth in personality and individuality.

Truth is simple, it can be found through patience and unselfishness. People turn outward to the Creator seeking something grand like a miracle. They do not realize truth is within them.

All of the prophets have preached this in one way or another. Give up self and enter into the holy way.

Religion must end and unselfishness must begin in order to witness peace and divinity.

The outer world partakes in warfare and ceaseless unrest. This is a direct result of the human heart and mind being filled with sin and evil. There is no such thing as devil. All evil, sin and sickness is manifested through man's mortal mind.

"Religion is not the Creators doing. It is the manifestation of personality and individuality. Every time I come across someone and they ask if I believe in God I tell them, "Yes, but I don't believe in religion". They then begin to ramble on about their faith and how in so many words if you don't believe in what they believe in then you're not going to heaven according to the Bible, Qur'an or whatever other scripture they follow. They believe their God is the lord of all, people, animals and things. But he only watches over those within their faith. The simplicity of the religious fanatics thinking never ceases to amaze me."

Look not in the mirror for self, for you are not the image you see. Your body is a vehicle which you utilize on this physical plain. The divine with you, meaning the God within you, is your real self. Humans are spirits created in likeness to the most high. You must reach within yourself.

You must give up sin and the beast within you. And you can only do this by realizing and living truth. It is very simple, let go of self and personality, and seek to build a better world for the glory of God within yourself so that it can be manifested in the material world. One word, LOVE, makes all this possible.

Once you've set upon the task of building yourself up from within, it is now time to seek to Manifest that which exists on the outer world. This will enable you to do all your labor to become all you can possibly be.

You are not robbing or taking from someone else that which is theirs. Instead you will be meditating upon and creating from mind and your thoughts to give form to that which you seek. Think what you seek into existence. Stop worrying about what the next individual has.

There is no need to seek to take from or compete with anyone. You can have that which you seek yourself. And it will only belong to you not anyone else. Wealth is meant for everyone. Poverty and the sacrifice of self without regard for the duty of your labor and what it brings to the building of the Creators Temple is not what he seeks. All souls have a task, and all must fulfill their duties and obligations. Knowledge, wisdom, understanding and material wealth are just some of the tools necessary for men to be able to become all they can become. All that's asked of you is gratitude. Sacrifice and rituals aren't necessary. Love in all its degrees is more than plentiful.

You cannot achieve great things until you begin to think in a great way.

Your fate is a direct result of your thoughts and actions. Even though this is so it is very possible for a sound thinking individual to change their fate. It is very possible to make a mistake, retrace your steps and rectify your thoughts and actions to produce totally different results. Only the learned that have come to know themselves and the Maker possess this talent.

There is no limit to man's potential. There has been no man who has lived who was so intelligent or spiritual that there hasn't been a man to come after him who has more intelligence or spirituality. You can draw from the knowledge and accomplishments of others to develop greater things than them. From the past days of ships made from wood now exists ships made from the finest and strongest metals. All this has been achieved by men building upon the insight and achievements of others.

The world like you is a thing that is constantly becoming. From lifeless form came existence in the physical plain, from one cell organisms to greater organisms. Nature was molded by the power of the Creator, starting from the simplest form to the complex. Everything is advancing and becoming. And it is the individual who is constantly aware of their thoughts who is able to tap into the higher consciousness and thus create and control their conditions and circumstances.

"Looking in the mirror I'm automatically reminded of how I've evolved from a teen wearing dreadlocks, army gear and urban wear. By my mid-twenties I cut the dreadlocks and began getting the hair corn rowed. I still wore urban wear, but no longer did I don army fatigues, etc.

By the time I reached thirty I started to keep my hair cropped short, choosing to wear soft bottom shoes, jeans and slacks and buttoned down shirts. Now I keep a Caesar or baldy, rarely ever wear sneakers and am wearing most of the time slacks and shoes. Each look changed with the environment and types of people I associate with, along with my occupation, etc. As I became more of who I wanted to become I found the need to change the way I think and look to adapt."

Humans since the beginning of time have been faced with the dilemma as to who they should serve.

There are many who labor unselfishly to help others. Many in doing so never become who they are truly meant to be. All their time, efforts and intelligence are spent in the service of others.

Others spend their days and nights in religious work, concerning themselves with rituals and intellectual talk about their faith. Our Creator whishes no one to sacrifice themselves or slave over others. Each of us possesses the light of the most high within us. All healthy thinking individuals have the capabilities to reach greatness. Our Creator is not concerned about rituals or sacrifices. There is nothing that man can give the Creator that our Master doesn't already possess. Our Master seeks to express himself through the work of humans. So if an individual truly wishes to serve than the only they need to do is live, and strive to be the greatest individual they can be. Find your purpose and learn how to do your labor in such a way that no one else can duplicate because, what you do is in such a great way. This is how you serve God.

Be true to yourself and in doing this it is impossible to be a liar to anyone else. In your immediate circle of family and friends be honest, true, unselfish, and humble. Strive to be the same way in all your dealings with people. Become this person in your mind, and meditate upon it until you become this person. Have faith in yourself and the ability to find truth and what the Creator desires from you.

Do not worry about changing into this great individual only to be faced with the wickedness of others. No healthy thinking man can be deprived of what he desires. In a free world no individual can be a slave to another unless they accept the individual as being their greater. And no individual is greater than the next, so never think this thought. To do so is to enslave yourself.

Nothing in the world can possibly alter who you are. You are the only person who can alter your thinking, actions and fate. All other changes which you perceive to be negative are really your own useless negative perceptions. Thoughts which you need to grow out of, and will as time progresses and you become more in tune with your true self and truth.

Wicked individuals whether kings, evil employers or politicians have power over individuals solely because people allow them to. There is no other reason at all. No man no matter what mental, spiritual or physical trickery they employ is suited to control another. No man possesses spirituality or intellectuality at such a level where no other man can learn and employ such gifts at a greater level than them. You were created to grow in intelligence. The world around you was created to assist your growth.

"When I was a youth I would look at older people who dedicated their lives to working and living honestly. Now after working all those years they struggle financially. It's this perception of life which fueled me toward a life of crime and dishonesty. I related strength and being strong with doing whatever you have to do to get yours. Even if this meant me living a life of crime. It never occurred to me that just as a person chooses to labor in a factory they could of chose to become an entrepreneur, white collar professional, business executive, lawyer, doctor or any other professional which will allow them the freedom to make enough financially to live on plus save for retirement. This way they would not have to struggle like the average American does when they retire. As I began to pursue my own life desires, travel and experience it helped me to see that no healthy thinking man within a free democratic world can be forced to be a slave to any man, place or institution without their consent."

It is easy to see everyone as your equal when you're not judgmental of others or meddling in their personal affairs. It is none of your business how a person thinks or lives. As long as how they think and live doesn't hinder you in any way you shouldn't be concerned. Mind your business and learn to want for others the same as you want for yourself.

Time after time you will be tested but you must have faith in the Creator and your own ability to control your conditions and circumstances.

Unfavorable situations may come forth, yet it is not what happens to you that affects you, it's more so how you view what happens to you that makes all the difference. So perception is the key. You must have faith in your inner self and the Creator. All things are becoming and move forward and stay focused on just this no matter what unfavorable circumstances arise. You have no responsibility or power to keep anyone right, or on the right path besides yourself. Once you become firm in your conviction of truth and vision you will automatically empower yourself.

47

Your mind will broaden and continue to do so as you travel down the road deeper into truth. Be patient and do not put more on yourself than you can handle or accomplish. Only do that which you can do in a great way. To undertake duties or challenges that you're not prepared to take is equivalent to walking across a busy road without looking for traffic.

If you seek to become great than learn to think in a great way.

Think about things which will enrich your life, not issues which the enslaved concern themselves with. There is more to life than just money, sex and physical possessions. Freedom, Justice and Equality as well as Love, Peace and Happiness are truths which most ignore yet depend on daily whether they realize it or not. Most concern themselves only when it's obvious they're being treated unfairly or their rights are being deprived. Then they cry out in vain because the universe does not reward truth to those who don't recognize or represent truth.

Selfish individuals only care about themselves. What happens to the next individual doesn't concern them. The circumstances don't matter whether it's life or death (it's unimportant). As long as they or their loved ones weren't involved it's all that matters. Now if the evil face of injustice were to visit them, all of the sudden they become patriots of the golden rule. "Do unto others that which you would like done to yourself."

"One morning while I was taking the train from my native Long Island, NY to Brooklyn I had the opportunity to overhear two gentleman talk about how in the state of New Jersey if you live outside the city or town limits within certain areas you have to pay a monthly fee for fire department services in order for them to assist you. I believe one family missed a payment of $75.00 one month and their house caught on fire. The fire department showed and watched the house burn down. They watched a half million dollar house burn to the dust. The fire chief when questioned by newspaper reporters stated it was the families fault for not paying their monthly premium. He also mentioned that more houses would burn down the same way. The man showed no conscience. He didn't care and doesn't care that a home may be everything a person owns. The suffering the family experienced didn't move him at all. But if you were to place him and his family in the same situation he'd more than likely feel the same way the family felt. Whatever energy you let out into the universe will revisit you sooner or later. The pain will surely be his one day."

Love and compassion is the truth men have sought since the beginning of time.

The truth is the Holy Grail, the knights of the round table have sought, traveling to distant lands only in the end to perish seeking that which they possessed since birth. The lack of Love is the reason for all the suffering humanity faces at the hands of themselves and other humans.

Love all but apply your wishes only upon yourself. No man has the ability to will upon another, whether it be for their benefit or not. Think and apply by utilizing only positive thoughts to form visions of what you seek. From this power all that you wish will be formed. There's no need to be jealous of the next individual. And there is definitely no point in assuming that you cannot accomplish what the next person has, and therefore it's necessary that you scheme and plot to obtain what they possess. The only limitations a man possesses are the ones he places upon himself. So do not worry about what material possessions an individual has trekked upon. To do so will cause you to think thoughts and undertake actions that will only bring pain your way.

What goes around comes around.

Unfortunately in these modern times where materialism and monetary wealth in many cases empowers or enslaves individuals a man can never be truly powerful without money.

The person who doesn't possess money no matter how smart they are more than not is at the mercy of the individual who possesses money. The sphere of the non-material is another matter.

Here nothing a man possesses means anything unless he represents eternal truth.

No matter who you are or your capabilities people will wonder as to your financial status.

Most people are more welcoming to individuals they feel are financially secure. They will welcome you to their homes, civic and religious functions, and many business opportunities will be passed onto you. You can be the most spiritual person in the world, a glowing light can be radiating around you for everyone to see. Let the average person know you are penniless and they will care not about your glowing. He will want very little to do with you. You can be a man of great ability and talent. But if you're poor individuals more financially fortunate than yourself will seek to utilize your talents to benefit their cause. They will use you and treat you with no equality because you're in need of their financial assistance of employ.

Monetary wealth just like knowledge, wisdom and understanding is a necessary tool in order to be powerful, independent and self-sufficient. You will not be able to develop or obtain the tools around you necessary for you to become all of who you are and are meant to be without material wealth.

Material Riches may not be the first thing you seek upon the road to freedom and eternal truth. But somewhere along your trek the accumulation of financial wealth must be sought to carry out your labor.

"Money may not be everything. But it took money to start my publishing company and every other venture I started. As an entrepreneur I realize that capital is just as important to a business and an individuals personal freedom as knowledge. Clearly when I've had money I've been in a better situation to do what I wanted to do then when I didn't have capital."

There is a saying that goes, "No man is an island." There is also one which states, "Two or more minds are better than one."

Once you find truth and come to a decision as to how you will serve God, yourself, and humanity it will be necessary to form an alliance with others to create a "think tank". Seek individuals who have your best interest in mind. Write down your goals and objectives. Your ultimate aim should be kept to yourself from possible traitors. Copies should be made and given to everyone who is a part of your alliance. All should sign; you should keep a copy and give each one back.

You should pray, if you believe in doing so, at least once every 24hrs. With the objectives of your missionary goal statement in mind, if your able to have all your alliance available for a moment of prayer everyday this would be great. If not seek to have at least one of them read off the missionary goal statement to you once a day.

If anyone is found to be disloyal or wavering in their belief of the missionary statement you remove them at once from your alliance. At all costs you must keep those who don't believe in your goals and objectives outside of your immediate person, and even away from you if possible.

You cannot succeed if people are working against you. Negative thoughts are the first stage of negative action.

On the outside of your circle of friends and associates do not be afraid of a little bit of opposition.

Adversity brings to the strong and determined success. It is only through opposition that you learn to truly value that which you possess. Never be ashamed to earn, for it is those who work and sacrifice that deserve.

Always seek to associate yourself with individuals who've established success. You can provide services and earn capital and invaluable insight under the protection of their knowledge and wisdom obtained through experience.

Individuals in a greater position than yourself have the ability to energize you with enthusiasm.

And enthusiasm has a way of recharging your mind and body, which enables you to eagerly you work toward goals. This is especially so if the individual is engaged in work they like.

Never fear failure because for the thinking and driven man it is only temporary.

Temporary failure is ones training so as to prepare you to be able to sidestep obstacles and jump over hurdles.

One must have the ability to fall, lick their wounds, get up and keep on walking.

"In reading biographies and autobiographies I've learned that some of the most notorious entrepreneurs have failed miserably several times until they found success. And in most cases they learned to associate themselves with individuals driven just like themselves, or folks who were already successful. In my case early on I took on the interest of reading about extraordinary figures so I can from a distance learn from them. I've also begun to make a practice of only hiring professionals who provide services who have a proven track record."

In your daily life amongst self, family, job or business it is most important to not lose sight of our objective to find truth (LOVE) and live it out daily in all that we do. You can obtain all the riches in the world, yet remember always that this experience is only temporary. Life is eternal, this is true but we are here for a purpose as humans, and then each soul has its own destiny as well which must be sought. We have a lifetime to figure it out, and we will not witness freedom until we let go of that which burdens us. Until you do so you will suffer lifetimes for thoughts and actions you partake in, and that which you thought about and partook in the past. Yes, some of the hardships you witness in this life are due to karma you face for things you've done in the previous life. Individuality and personality and the "I and Me" persona are the reason men hate, lust and envy.

Free is the individual who learns to LOVE all.

He or she will join the ranks of those who know eternal truth. They will have risen from child, to manhood/womanhood to godhood to sit amongst the other gods and the One God.

TRUTH

The Truth is not trapped in words. It derives from the source of all truth. It echoes within all time and space and vibrations within all plains of life. The truth is in all as it originated all. The only Man who knows Truth is the one who lives according to Truths principles.

With millions of years of mans history behind us to stare upon, yet unrest exists it would not be unfair to ask the question, "Where does truth lie?" The Christians condemn the Muslims. The Muslims do the same in regards to the Christians. The Protestants and Catholics debate over doctrines and interpretations. The Baptists, Methodists and other denominations of Christianity look toward one another as strangers and liars of the Word because of interpretations and rituals.

Where peace and accord should exist there is only strife and confusion. Individuality and Personality is one place where religion surely dwells. Whether with closed eyes or open one must acknowledge that individuality and personality is the undoer and destroyer of humans.

Religion is the work of the mortal mind and serves the needs of sects, and groups of people residing in regions where people gravitate toward the idea of separatism to serve their own need.

Our Creator is all and in all, and there are no separations. He is the truth in all spheres of existence whether material or non material. He is the Master of all upon all continents, oceans and seas and the air. None who claims separation from others, or other life forms serves him or his purpose.

All are imposters and deceivers of themselves first and foremost. A man who lies to self lies to all. Knowledge of self is the foundation to all other knowledge including the knowledge of the Omnificent.

Holiness is the only true peace. It is the work and application of good virtues. If one applies themselves unselfishly and diligently to let go of self and walk away from sin in its various forms, then they will witness peace in it all its degrees. All other self gratification which bring about peace, manifest a peace which is only temporary. Once strife and confusion enter such peace disappears. An individual rooted in peace is like a boulder standing amongst terrible winds, swaying trees, and branches, yet the boulder stands firm and un-removed amongst all the confusion.

Humans being spirit and body dwell within the realms of material and non material. It's this duality which drives and also imprisons mankind. Like waves crashing the physical world drowns in conflict. Yet within humans exist light, peace, and comfort on a scale far grandeur than can be found within this physical world. It is when a man goes inside himself that peace and tranquility can be found no matter where he stands, or whom he stands amongst.

Amongst all the chaos mankind still searches for comfort and believes that somewhere eternal peace does exist. Only those who succumb 100% to the divine power within can find peace. One can go to the church, mosque, temple or any other religious institution several times a day. One can practice rituals religiously on the hour every day. All this will serve no true benefit if one is not in accord with the holy place within themselves.

If you can find peace for any moment of your life it is surely possible for you to find peace for eternity. It is truly up to you how your life plays out. You are the maker of your own fate. This is the gift the Creator has bestowed upon mankind. It is the truth, which allows us in the face of unthinkable sin to keep faith in the reality that through the knowledge of God and application of good virtues all good will come full circle.

Meditate upon the truth, let go of self and your prejudices and seek the truth only. In time you will begin to free yourself from all negative thoughts and emotions that you've learned in the past. With patience and time peace will come to you. Set aside a time of the day for meditation and keep a daily schedule and time set aside just for this purpose. We are what we repeatedly think and do.

Sin, disease and sickness are not a product of Truth or the Creator. Illness and negative emotions are manifested by the mortal mind, man's lower self, lower consciousness. You are what you repeatedly think and do. That which you fear can very well become your reality. If you constantly fix your mind on disease and illness then it's very possible that you do take ill. This is an unfortunate fate, but nevertheless is brought about by your own thoughts. Think of health and prosperity, and good and prosperity will be yours to experience.

Truth is universal. Within the collective unconsciousness lies the truth of all ages. All that we discover today confirms truths of the past. Millions of years of human history lie within the records of collective consciousness. The amazing point is that it is available for those who are bold enough to seek.

Without truth we are nothing. All that we do will be undone, incomplete and unbalanced without the foundation of Truth to stand upon. Mankind coming together in spirit and harmony is the power, which has driven us to build forth in Truth and the glory of the Creator. What will become of us? Will all that was left to us go to waste because we chose to be ruled by Self instead of our Creator? All the great men and women that are spoken of within history books, biographies, autobiographies and countless other volumes of works are they to look upon us in shame? Are we not to finish their work or at least continue where they left off? Surely after our bones go back to dust and our spirits are released from the body we shall cross their paths. Shall we be ashamed?

It doesn't matter what worldly feats you have appeared to accomplish when your heart, mind and soul is not rooted in Love for all that you are and all that you're a part of. Surely you must at some point realize that mankind is rooted in every element of the universe from which we were molded from and out of. It doesn't matter that you live in a mansion, have a large salary, a college degree, and belong to a prestigious country club. Are you a good person? Are you fair and caring to all those you come across? Do you take without giving or do you partake in community up building for all that you've been blessed with. Are you a good person? If you're controlled by personality, individuality, are jealous, hateful, greedy or deviant, all that you appear to be here on earth will mean nothing when your time to pass on to the next stage comes. All those who do not come into Truth will face karma and a worse life then they just witnessed. All will be repeated until one decides to walk in Truth. One has a whole lifetime to get it right. No one shall or can cheat; the laws of the universe are unbreakable. We have the ability to make choices for ourselves. But this gift was bestowed upon us so that we can utilize the tools we were born with (intelligence, spirit, body) to create and mold for the up building of this physical world and the inner self. All those who have achieved such building of the Holy Temple sit as gods amongst the company of God.

In the midst of industrialization and the desire of power and wealth in the material realm mankind's head has been taken from the body. In other words, mankind has set itself on a course to act in opposition to itself. Instead of intelligence being used as a vehicle to build the outer world, and therefore also build the inner self passion and ambition has been let loose to rule.

Passion and ambition has killed intelligence, and therefore has separated the head from the body.

Humans cry for peace amongst all the peace and terror. They await for a messiah to return or be resurrected when it is they whom can save themselves. It has always been so. Once their minds are no longer ruled by their own passions and desires and other humans they will possess the power to free and save themselves. They must first build from within and seek Truth. From this change a healthy thinking man or woman can change any circumstance they face. It is Truth that can conquer all.

The leaders are corrupt, yet are also only a reflection of the humans they lead. The people are corrupt and lack truth and therefore select leaders who are rooted in the same filth. The people in turn get the leaders they deserve. Since the people are not rooted in good character and virtues they take not the time to study the individual running for office. Instead they listen to fancy words and well put together sentences and speeches. The officials rob and loot once they obtain position. Shockingly the people act as if they were deceived just because they heard the words of what appeared to be a sincere and honest person upon the campaign trail. Actions speak louder than words, and history is the best teacher. If you would like to know a man all you have to do is study the history of his actions. How can a man who has been a liar and deceiver for quite some time all of the sudden be a changed man overnight? Humans are creatures of habit. That which we do the most becomes a part of us. And that which we think of the most becomes the fuel to set fire to action.

"I myself am a reformed man of a criminal nature. I just didn't wake up and become a drug dealer, robber, gun man, etc. These thoughts were lodged deep within my psyche long before I took action. Everyone I knew who had material wealth and was young was doing some type of dirt. For a while I just sat back and watched.

That which I thought about most I became. On the flipside when I decided to change my life for the better it wasn't an overnight process at all. It was something I first pondered about for a while. Mentally gradually I became the good person who I wanted to become. And little by little I took action to form the habit. No individual becomes good or a sinner overnight. Like with all things there's a process."

Truth is of the Creator and there are many paths that lead to truth. Man through becoming better men, and walking in and practicing good virtues are surely to find themselves at the same point in the end.

Human babies are bathed in truth. They know not right from wrong. It is when they are exposed to the lies and negative thoughts of those around them that they are ushered into the ways of the mortal mind and the world. Every day as they live they lose more and more of their true nature of being bathed in truth. As adults they stare into the mirror believing that which they see is actually who they are. It is only the conscious individual who understands the path that led them to the stage of death, dumb, and blind also leads back to the Holy Temple if they were to retrace their steps. But first one must renounce the ways of the world and the type of thinking which tore down the sanctuary within.

The Truth is the treasure wars have been fought over. It is the Holy Grail King Arthurs Knights searched for. It is the secret treasure the Knights Templar left behind. It is the glory all modern religions speak of. All of the things which man has plundered others for, set out on great expeditions in search of, built many religious institutions and monuments to worship, acknowledge and spend countless hours in utter despair, and ignorance. Most humans know not the truth. They assume it's some very complicated equation beyond their comprehension, so it's better to walk in blind faith. Like zombies they walk here and there pretending they are looking.

But the truth is they wish not to find the truth. They don't want to be responsible. Like children they want to be absolved of all responsibility for their thoughts and actions, lives and well being of others. An ignorant person cannot be held responsible for what they think or do. But when something is revealed to you, you are bonded to it, and therefore bare the brunt of responsibility.

The truth is as close to you as your jugular vein. It is within you no different than the heart beating blood inside of you. LOVE is what holds this whole universe together working as one. And if it is Love that is the Truth.

Search no more!

SELF

On a daily basis humans look here and there for the enemy. Never do they acknowledge that as adults it's been and is their own decisions which have brought them in the midst of the wrong people, places, conditions and circumstances. Ones emotions, desires, wants and selfishness drive them down the roads of suffering and despair like a drunkard behind the wheel of a car. If you allow Self to Rule. If you allow your Lower Kingdom to have control then War is all you'll ever witness. Your days and nights will be spent Running. The Creator and Higher Conscious will forever whisper to you. It's this Truth which slowly kills many driving them to drink, do drugs and act in a manner that only serves to further destroy themselves.

When you stare into a mirror and see the physical image you may falsely assume that which you see is yourself. If you were to touch this physical composition it would take a sure understanding of the essence of who you are to not say to yourself, "I feel cold, or I'm hurting" because since birth you've been brainwashed to think that the physical world and all that's in it is actual, instead of a mirror, reflection, vehicle and temple to house or transport energy within the material realm. To transport means to take or move from one place to another. In other words this material world is but temporary -it is not permanent. Energy doesn't die;

69

it transforms itself from one stage to another. So life is eternal. Therefore it is impossible for that which you witness within this physical world to be all and everything that you shall witness. Humans and all other matter in this physical realm in essence are of non material or of the spirit realm. It is now that you're having an earthly experience.

All matter evolves overtime from infancy to a progressive state of maturity. The human spirit is the oldest and most developed of all others. Mineral, plant and animal are states of existence humans have witnessed at one time or another before reaching a state where intelligence, consciousness and self control were developed on a level to the image of the Creator.

Like children birthed from the mothers womb the spirit which has evolved over time from all stages of mineral, plant and animal matter now into that spirit to which becomes housed into the human body. From here consciousness is awoke within the vessel like a light bulb being turned on in a house. The Creator recreates a level of itself giving this earthly being the power to evolve in consciousness and awareness and tap into the supreme consciousness of the Creator through education and self awareness as it develops from infancy to adulthood. It beholds the power to become at one with the Creator if it so seeks.

70

For humans knowledge of self is the foundation to all other knowledge. All matter contained within the physical universe is contained within the physical composition of humans. Humans at one point within the physical realm evolved from mineral, plant and animal existence to maturity. Therefore that which humans evolved from also exists within their DNA make-up.

This also shows and proves that all life matter is connected to one another, and also to one life source, order and chain of command.

Unlike nature and animal instinct humans are enabled with the ability to reach a state of existence where they can control their conditions and circumstances. Humans have a responsibility to educate themselves and bring to consciousness and light the awareness of themselves and the world around them, which will enable them to expand their consciousness and the world outside of themselves. If humans fail to educate themselves and those young ones entrusted to them than they who stand without knowledge of self, and who do not possess the ability to build their consciousness or add on to the development of the world are no better than beasts in the field.

It is self awareness and the ability to build oneself from within to further develop the human spirit and the

71

outer world which causes humans to be drastically different than mineral, plant or animal life.

Once humans develop their consciousness to a level of self awareness and development the next stage is to build outside of oneself that which exists within. All labor taken upon with Love is a direct result of the Love one possesses within themselves. And all things built with Love are sure to be built upon a solid foundation. The man/woman who comes to understand that the outer and inner world are one in the same then has the ability to move further into a deeper awakening of consciousness. Some call this next stage godhood. This is the existence spoken about in the Bible when the use of the term Son of man is mentioned. Man meaning Mind and Mind meaning God or Supreme Intelligence. Son referring to the man who actively develops his consciousness and actions in a manner which betters himself, his fellow humans and the world. He becomes a builder of the kingdom within and out. His destiny is to sit with the others and the Creator. The others being those throughout the ages like himself who have actively rose above the confines of the claims of the mortal mind, and the physical composition the spirit is encased within.

It's in the awareness that life is but a series of events encompassing many stages of existence, non material and material that awakes thee to a need to find purpose in the reason for development from the minute organism to the stage of human development and consciousness. It is here that one finds a bond with all other life matter as an elder to other life forms. One realizes that through humans the Creator experiences life in this material plain. It is the reason and cause for mankind to build, and build forth greater today than they did yesterday, and tomorrow greater than the present. The world is constantly becoming as a man becomes in the image of the Creator, and as the Mind of the Creator seeks to become.

THOUGHT BUILDING EXERCISE

According to Biblical dictionaries, the essence of Man is the Holy Ghost. It is also acknowledged that the Holy Ghost is the Mind as it is a reflection of the Creator who is the source of all knowledge. By building your mind, you're building your consciousness. And in doing this you're becoming more and more like the source of all Consciousness.

The choices we make dictate the life we live. When I was in my early twenties I became fascinated with the subjects of psychology and politics. I became aware of the reality of "think tanks" and their use by governments, organizations both governmental and in the business sector. These are individuals brought together for a Cause and from their psychology and occupational expertise they predict possible outcomes. Through analysis they then narrow down the possible outcomes or Effects to produce the one they need. These groups are usually composed of psychologists, sociologists, scientists, doctors, government or company officials, etc. The bottom-line is that in most cases these individuals are experts within their profession, and getting the results they seek.

The exercise I'm bringing to the forefront has to do with you deciding what it is that you want, and getting exactly this by narrowing down the outcomes. The first thing you need to do is create the Cause or spark to set it all in motion. The Effect is the result or outcome obtained. As with all Cause there is a possibility to obtain many results or Effects. Some of these can be the totally opposite of what you seek. While others can come close to what you seek but not be exactly what you want.

The objective is to obtain the exact results you desire. Contrary to popular belief there is no such thing as luck or things just coming about. All Effects are the product of Cause. Math is the only precise science in the universe and in math you cannot get anything from zero. Math is a universal language and science is connected to the foundation of all matter; material and non material.

Think about what you want, make a decision as to what you want and then set the ball in motion. Well, instead of being in such a rush to do and obtain results lets take the time to THINK. Take the time to not just think about what it is that you want. But instead of taking action to obtain what you want, think every step through first so you can narrow down to a precise degree the results you'll obtain.

1. Think about what you want.

2. Decide if you have the knowledge and faculties to obtain what you want.

3. If you do not possess the necessary knowledge and faculties to obtain what you want then take the time to obtain them before moving forward.

4. If you have the necessary tools then get a notebook, jot down what you seek, then what actions it will take to obtain what you want, and who will be involved in bringing about the cause.

5. Next decide the possible outcome of the action(s) taken. In other words decide all possible results. Write each one down on a separate line.

6. Go through all the possible negative outcomes and think each one through with the focus on how you can take an action that will make it impossible for this result to take place.

Go through each one and do the same thing, until you're sure that it would almost be an impossibility for you to obtain an unfavorable result.

7. Now that you've thought all the negative outcomes through take a look at all the positive ones. Think about how you can take action to bring about more positive results if at all possible.

8. Go through your list from 1-7 once over reviewing every item in your mind and on paper once again. Now you're ready to play it out in real life.

The best thing any human can do is Think, for without thought fate is at the mercy of reckless action.

PROFILE YOURSELF

One of the greatest things any human can do to ensure they're getting the most out of themselves is to constantly evaluate themselves. This means to study on a consistent basis, apply what you learn in everyday life, and take notes of the results. Every now and then take a break to see where you're at in reference to where you want to go.

Knowledge of self is the foundation to all other knowledge. Learning about yourself is the single most important thing anyone can do. Building a profile of yourself will help you realize your strong and weak points and provide you with a starting point from which to build from. After all nothing remains the same; all things are governed by change, either for the better or worse.

Develop a list of points and define each the best you can:

1. Who are you? In other words, what makes you the person that you are?
2. What is it that you care about most?
3. What are your best mental qualities?
4. What are your worst mental qualities?
5. What are your religious and spiritual beliefs? Why?

6. Are you your own person or are you made by others?
7. What can you do to make yourself a more complete person?
8. Are the people around you supportive? Do they bring about the best in you?
9. Are you engaged in the occupation you desire?
10. Are you taking the necessary steps to obtain the education and expertise you need to engage in the occupation you desire?

11. Do you have written out detailed short term and long term goals?
12. If you do are you following through every day with your goals?
13. Do you make a habit of practicing good virtues?
14. Do you treat others the same way you would like to be treated?
15. Is the supreme power at the center of all you do?

Made in the USA
Middletown, DE
16 October 2016